Adwoba Addo-Boateng

Emails to God
By
Adwoba Addo-Boateng

Adwoba Addo-Boateng

Emails to God
Adwoba Addo-Boateng

Published by Parables
April 2020

All Rights Reserved. No part of this book may be reproduced or utilized in any form or by any means, electronic or mechanical, including photocopying, recording, or by any information storage and retrieval system, without permission in writing from the author.

ISBN **9781951497446**
Printed in the United States of America

Readers should be aware that Internet Web sites offered as citations and/or sources for further information may have been changed or disappeared between the time this was written and the time it is read.

Emails to God

By

Adwoba Addo-Boateng

Adwoba Addo-Boateng

Dedication

To Maame Nhyira Addo-Boateng, my lovely daughter.

This is truly girls' stuff.

I love you with all my heart.

Mummy.

Dear Readers,

A young girl called Self gets introduced to God by her mom. She decides to follow the trend by sending emails to God as a way of communicating to him.

They start a wonderful relationship. However, she faces many challenges, she loses her friends, but she finds God's love and extends it to others. She finds her true self and her girls' group is restored in a better way.

Adwoba Addo-Boateng

To: godmail.com
From: selfmail.com
Date: 15th March 2020
Subject: Introduction

Dear God,
I am self. My mum talks a lot about you, and she said I can talk to you too. So, I decided to send you emails. I hope that is cool. I am a teenager and I love girls' stuff but never really loved you. But let's see how this will work.
My dad is in the army and he is on a peace mission, so I really need someone to talk to everyday. My mom recommended you. Would you mind? Well today is the last day of the term and I would want us to plan something during this vacation.
P.S My mum is pregnant; I am excited about this.
Sincerely,
Self.

RE: Introduction
Hey Self,
I have always been your daddy in heaven watching over you. I am so excited to be your friend. I love friends. If you abide in me, then you are my friend, ask me anything you wish, and it will be done for you.
Let's toast to a wonderful relationship.
Kisses to the bump.

God

To: godmail.com
From: selfmail.com
Date: 16th March 2020
Subject: Question

Dear God,
I have a nice home; I have this cute hairstyle and I am blessed! Did you give me all that?

Self.

RE: QUESTION

Dear Self,
Every good and perfect gift is from above coming down from the Father of lights who does not change like shifting shadows. (James 1:17 NIV).

Enjoy!

God

To: godmail.com
From: selfmail.com
Date: 17th March 2020
Subject: More about me

Dear God,
So, I belong to this girls' group and we analyze crazy things like how out of fashion, Mandy's hair looked yesterday. We argue about when to text a crush or post a selfie.

Unfortunately, my mum thinks it is EVIL, but it is not. It is rather a good way to share ideas.

Let me know your thoughts.

Self.

RE: More about me

Dear Self,
Thank you so much for sharing with me. There is nothing bad in being in a girls' group however what the focus of the group is, is what matters.

Suggestion: Tell them about me.

I love you,

God.

To: godmail.com
From: selfmail.com
Date: 18th March 2020
Subject: Update

Dear God,
You know, I like to look pretty. I LOVE my hair. Can you get me a jacket I saw at the shop the last time? It is the latest fashion. It has two silver zips at the side, and I will really look cute in it.

Hoodies! I need one so bad.

Being a teenage girl is filled with ups and downs and tons of sadness at that time of the month.

Self.

RE: UPDATE

Dear Self,
Life is not a bed of roses. There are ups and downs in everything, however I never change, so put your trust in me.

Let's see about that Jacket.

God.

To: godmail.com
From: selfmail.com
Date: 19th March 2020
Subject: Sleepover

Dear God,
My friends are having a sleepover at my house today. We are going to have so much fun. Oh, how we love to mess around in those flowery pajamas. My friends suggested we talk about boys but seriously I don't want to. Since, we began talking, I so want to talk about you every day.

Self.

RE: Sleepover

Dear Self,
It's great your friends are coming over. It will be great to talk about me and encourage them to have a relationship with me too.

Take Care

God.

To: godmail.com
From: selfmail.com
Date: 20th March 2020
Subject: Update on Sleepover

Dear God,
We had a wonderful time, but my friends wouldn't eat anything at dinner time. They get stressed about food. They do not eat for fear of getting fat.

I spoke to them about you. My friends said following you is so boring. But I told them it is so much fun.

Self.

RE: Update on Sleepover

Dear Self,
I knew you will have a great time. Keep on telling your friends about me.

Love you,

God

To: godmail.com
From: selfmail.com
Date: 22nd March 2020
Subject: Just to let you know

Dear God,
I scored A in all my tests this term. I am a straight A student, but creative writing is my passion.

I have a crush on this tall boy in my class. He stares at me all the time and I think I like him too, but mummy thinks it is too early to date.

I only have one hour left before I sleep.
Waiting for your reply.
Self.

RE: just to let you know

Dear Self,
I think you should consider getting good grades for now and pursuing your passion.

Love you,

God.

To: godmail.com
From: selfmail.com
Date: 23rd March 2020
Subject: I am on vacation

Dear God,
This term was very tedious. There were loads and loads of exercises but thankfully we were able to sail through.
Since I am on vacation, I want a job to get busy. My friends don't want to be with me anymore, they say I am acting weird these days. I am always talking about you. But that is what I crave for.

Please help me!

Counting on you
Yours Sincerely,
Self.

RE: I am on vacation

Dear Self,
How beautiful are the feet of those who bring good news! (Romans 10:15 NIV). I will grant your request for a job soon.

Take care.

Sincerely,

God

To: godmail.com
From: selfmail.com
Date: 24th March 2020
Subject: Waiting on God

Dear God,
I have been waiting for the job you promised me, and I am so tired of waiting. Do I still have to keep on waiting?
Sincerely,
Self.

RE: Waiting on God

Dear Self,
I understand, waiting can be hard but waiting in the Lord for his will to be done at the right time is the perfect thing to do. Wait patiently by constantly abiding in him so that your mind will be renewed according to what God wants to be done for you. (Romans 12:2 NIV).

My regards to your family.
All the best.
With Lots of Love,

God.

To: godmail.com
From: selfmail.com
Date: 25th March 2020.
Subject: I need a miracle

Dear God,
I seriously need a miracle; nothing seems to work. I really need the job.

Waiting anxiously for your reply.
Sincerely,
Self.

RE: I need a miracle

Dear Self,
I noticed a lot of anxiety in your last email. Please do not be anxious about anything, present your request to the Lord so that the peace of God will guard your heart and mind in Christ Jesus. (Philippians 4:6-7)
I am sending peace over to you, you need it and of course I am sending the Holy Spirit to help you. I am sure, you will be just fine.
Be calm.
God is with you.
All the best,

God.

To: godmail.com
From: selfmail.com
Date: 26th March 2020
Subject: I am worried

Dear God,
I am very worried about life and the fact that you are not giving me my job.
Please help me God.

RE: I am worried
Dear Self,
Sometimes in life, we do get worried but ask yourself; have you added a single hour to your life by worrying. I always tell you not to worry about your life, what you will eat or drink or about your body what you will wear. Life is more important than all these things.

Just look at the birds of the air; they do not sow or reap or store away in barns, and yet I feed them. Also, look at how the flowers of the field grow, they do not labor or spin, but I take care of them all. I am the good shepherd and a good shepherd takes care of his sheep. Have faith in me and seek ye first the kingdom of God and all other things will be added to it. (Matthew 6:26-31 NIV).
Stay composed.

Blessings,

God.

To: godmail.com
From: selfmail.com
Date: 27th March 2020
Subject: I am scared

Dear God,
Fear is crippling me these days for a reason I don't know. I get scared that I would not be able to go to college.
Please advise.
Self.

RE: I am scared
Fear is of the devil. You are just afraid of the unknown. Live in the known that Christ saves and that everything will work out for good for those who love the Lord and those who have been called according to his purpose (Romans 8:28 NIV).
Don't forget to dwell in my word.

I love you so much.

God.

To: godmail.com
From: selfmail.com
Date: 28th March 2020
Subject: I am bored

Dear God,
I am so bored; I just sit idle all the time. I am wearing a jumper today because I was too bored to wear a two- piece clothing.

Love,
Self

RE: I am bored
Dear Self,
The devil gives work for idle hands to do. Get soaked in the word for the Holy Spirit to direct you on what to do.

I will be waiting to hear what you have come up with.
Love Always,

God.

To: godmail.com
From: selfmail.com
Date: 29th March 2020
Subject: Compelled to give

Dear God,
I had always wanted to tell you about this. I was at Church last Sunday and I felt pressured to put money in the offertory bowl because everyone was doing it and truthfully sometimes it is not coming from my heart. I want to do the right thing, please I need your advice on this. Also, about the boredom, I spoke to you about the other time, the Holy Spirit helped me with some great idea. Guess what? I now spend time doing charity work at the community center. It is so great to help. I feel so fulfilled. Thank you so much for all your help.
Hoping to hear from you soon.
Self.

RE: Compelled to give
Dear Self,
Thank you for your honesty. These are the worshipers that I desire, worshipers who will worship me in spirit and in truth. You must give what you have decided in your heart to give, not reluctantly or in response to pressure. For I love a cheerful giver (2 Corinthians 9:7 NIV) Thank you for listening to the Holy Spirit. Loving people is one of my greatest commandments. I am happy to hear this.
Keep the light burning! God.

To: godmail.com
From: selfmail.com
Date: 30th March 2020
Subject: I finally had the job.

Dear God,
I was at the community center yesterday, when the owner of the shop down the street called me to be his assistant in a paint store. Apparently, he had also come to the community center to donate some paint. Did you know I would meet him there?

Anyway, I am starting work today. I am all dressed up and about leaving for work. I wish I had the Jacket to wear to work today.
I will give you updates!
Self.

RE: I finally had the job
Dear Self,
I am so happy; you finally have the job. So, you see how you thought about people and volunteered at the community center and voila you had the job.
Enjoy working!
Keep me posted,

God.

To: godmail.com
From: selfmail.com
Date: 31st March 2020
Subject: My boss is creepy

Hi God,
I love the job and the fact that I have to talk to people all the time, but my new boss is so creepy, and he gives me all the work to do whilst he walks about aimlessly during working hours.

In fact, I feel like punching him in the face sometimes.
Sincerely.
Self.

RE: My Boss is creepy
Dear Self,
Two wrongs do not make a right. Hey, what happened to working for your masters as if you are working for the Lord and the good Lord will reward you not your boss. Leave your boss out of this and set your mind on things above.
We shall talk more.
Till then,

God.

To: godmail.com
From: selfmail.com
Date: 1st April 2020
Subject: Tit for Tat?

Dear God,
I will be brief with this. A friend in the girls' group stabbed me in the back a few days ago and she was at the shop today. Now there is an opportunity to pay her back for her bad deeds. Should I go ahead paying her back for what she did to me back then?

Sitting on tenterhooks,
Self.

RE: Tit for Tat?
Dear Self,
I will be brief with this as well. If you love those who love you, what credit is that to you? Even sinners do that. And if you do good to those who are good to you, what credit is that to you, Even, sinners do that. Do good to those that treated you badly or hate you and your reward will be great. (Luke 6).
I hope you get this.

Counting on your co-operation.
P.S What are you doing on April fool's day?

God.

To: godmail.com
From: selfmail.com
Date: 2nd April 2020
Subject: He doesn't know God

Dear God,
A colleague at work is on drugs and I hate him so much. I feel he is dirty, and I don't want to get close to him. Please advise on what to do.

P.S earning money on your own is awesome.
Sincerely,
Self

RE: He doesn't know God
Dear Self,
Do not judge and you will not be judged. Do not condemn and you will not be condemned. (Luke 6 NIV). But watch and pray so that you also will not be tempted.

These are the people we should love as Christians and embrace them however they are. I have demonstrated my own love for you in this: while we were still sinners, Christ died for us (Romans 5:8) And the least you could do is to give that love back.
All the best,

God.

RE: RE: He doesn't know God

Dear God,

I know I must love him but anytime I try to tell him about you. He shuts me down. And I feel bad about that.

Self.

RE: RE: RE: He doesn't know God

Dear Self,
When people get addicted to drugs. The drugs take the place of God and they turn to drugs to help them instead of God.

The message of the cross is foolishness to those who are perishing but to those of us being saved it is the power of God (1 Corinthians 1:18 NIV).

Keep on sowing the seed, it might be fruitful someday and pray for him.

God.

To: godmail.com
From: selfmail.com
Date: 3rd April 2020
Subject: I fear getting sick.

Dear God,
How are you doing? I hope you are well. So, everyone has a flu in my house, and I am afraid of catching the flu.

I seriously don't want to catch this flu, because I can't afford to sit at home the whole day not working.

Thank you for your concern,
Self.

RE: I fear getting sick.

Dear Self,
Do you remember the story of the faith of the Centurion? That man had great faith. If you have forgotten read Matthew 8. You have little faith. If you have faith as small as a mustard seed, you can say to this mountain, move from here to there and it will move. Nothing will be impossible for you. (Matthew 17:20 NIV)

So, my dear, have faith in me and remember whatever I do, I do for your own good.
Love Always,

God.

To: godmail.com
From: selfmail.com
Date: 4th April 2020
Subject: Hello

Dear God,
I came to work a bit early today, so I am the only one in the shop. Yesterday, a colleague wanted me to record sales in the sales book when we have not sold anything. I felt this was bad and so I didn't do it. He started hurling insults at me. I really cried.

I wish I had never taken the job.
P.S Mummy is not feeling too well. Please heal her.

Love Always,
Self.

RE: Hello
Dear Self,
I just love you so much. The temptations will always come but when you are so rooted in me, the word overrides it. We are always tempted when we are dragged away by our own evil desire and enticed. This evil desire always leads to sin and sin destroys the relationship between you and me (James 1:14 NIV).
I am so proud of you girl. Your mother will be fine in no time.
Love you,

God

RE: RE: Hello

Dear God,

That was a swift reply. Initially, I didn't want to tell you this, but I guess I should. This same guy asked me to meet him in a secluded place this evening.
I really feel something bad might happen.
What do you think?

Self.

RE: RE: RE: Hello

Dear Self,
Yes, something bad will happen. Flee from sexual immorality. (1 Corinthians 6:18 NIV).

Take Care!

God

To: godmail.com
From: selfmail.com
Subject: Everyone does not like me
Date: 5th April 2020

Dear God,
Everyone hates me now at work and does not want to be friends with me because of my high moral values. Sometimes, I feel like joining the crowd.
Please help before I do something drastic.
Self.

RE: Everyone does not like me.

Dear Self,
This is something I wanted to tell you about when you decided to follow me. You will be hated because of me, but the one who stands firm will be saved (Matthew 10: 22 NIV).
Run your race with perseverance, fixing our eyes on Jesus, the pioneer and perfecter of our faith. (Hebrews 12)
I will be strengthening you during this period.
Do get in touch,

God.

To: godmail.com
From: selfmail.com
Date: 6th April 2020
Subject: No reply.

Dear God,
I have sent you numerous mails and you are not replying. Please reply my mails.
Thanks,
Self.

RE: No reply.
Dear Self,
I reply every mail you send. I am thinking sometimes because it is not the reply you need; it goes to spam. Please check all your spam emails and read them.
All the best,

God.

To: godmail.com
From: selfmail.com
Date: 7th April 2020
Subject: I made a new friend

Dear God,
I made a new friend; she is very much like me. We both love you. However, she doesn't know you, but she wants to know you. I will forward her mail to you.
Sincerely,
Self.

RE: I made a new friend
Dear Self,
I am glad you made a new friend. Remember to love her as much as you love yourself.

You can forward her mail to me but encourage her to send me mails herself.

P.S My email address is in her heart.

Happily,

God.

To: godmail.com
FW: friendsmail.com
Date: 8th April 2020
Subject: How can I find God?

Dear Self,
I just wish I can find God and talk to him every day, the way you have. I keep on searching for him, but I have not been able to find him. Can you please help me in finding God?
Keeping my fingers crossed,
Friend.

----- Forwarded Message -----
From: friend <friendmail.com>
To: "selfmail.com" <selfmail.com>
Sent: Friday, April 3, 2020, 11:03:53 PM EDT
Subject: How Can I find God?

RE: FW: friendsmail.com
Dear Friend,
I am closer to you than you think. You must open your heart and receive me first for as many as received me, or to those who believed in my name. I gave them the right to become children of God (John 1:12 NIV). Start an interpersonal relationship with me by talking to me every time, dwelling in my word and living in my love. let's see where it will take us.
Waiting for your next email.
XoXO

God.

To: godmail.com
From: selfmail.com
Date: 9th April 2020
Subject: I can't stop lying

Dear God,
I have been lying a lot lately because I want to cover up a lot of things. Let me tell you how it started, it was just one simple lie at work, and it has turned me something else.

I want to get out of this as quickly as I can. Please help!

Sincerely,
Self

RE: I can't stop lying
Dear Self,
When did this start? Anyway, if you are my child then you need to throw away every sin that entangles and lying is one of them. If you belong to your father, the devil then you would like to carry out his desires by not holding on to the truth.

I must be stern here; Submit yourselves, then, to God. Resist the devil, and he will flee from you (James 4:7 NIV). Let me know how this goes.
Your Father in Heaven.

God.

To: godmail.com
From: selfmail.com
Date: 10th April 2020
Subject: Reminder

Dear God,
Just a quick email to remind you of the jacket I asked you. It is taking too long.
And guess what? Your method worked perfectly; I have stopped lying.

P.S. I really want the jacket.

Love,
Self.

RE: Reminder

Dear Self,
Your heavenly father will give good gifts to those who ask him. Expect it in God's time (Matthew 7:10-12 NIV).

Sincerely,

God.

To: godmail.com
From: selfmail.com
Date: 11th April 2020
Subject: hello

Dear God,
I was just checking up on you.
I love you so much.
Love,
Self.

RE: hello.
Dear Self,
Thank you for checking up on me. These are some of the things that draws us closer to each other.
Remember, you have nothing to lose if you check on me always.
Remain blessed,

God.

To: godmail.com
From: selfmail.com
Date: 12th April 2020.
Subject: I am disappointed

Dear God,
This email is a bit harsh, but I can't help it. I am disappointed in you. I have followed you for a long time, but I have nothing to show for. You are still not giving me the Jacket! Not to talk of the hoodie. No offense, but I keep asking myself is it worth it following you?

Disappointed Self.

RE: I am disappointed
Dear Self,
Wow! I was not expecting this mail but if only for this life we have hope in Christ, we are of all people most to be pitied (1 Corinthians 15:19 NIV).

God.

To: godmail.com
From: selfmail.com
Date: 13th April 2020
Subject: Fight

Dear God,
My new friend and I fought today. She talked badly about me to her friend. I don't want to ever see her again.

Please can you give me a new friend?
Love,
Self.

RE: Fight
Dear Self,
These things are bound to happen. You are two different people coming from different backgrounds, there will certainly be differences.

Learn to let go and try and forgive her and be friends again.
The Holy Spirit will help you.

Counting on your co-operation.

God

To: godmail.com
From: selfmail.com
Date: 14th April 2020
Subject: I can't let go

Dear God,
I am so angry with my friend that I can't easily forgive her. I thought this friendship was going to last forever.

Anytime, I see her, she reminds me of the pain she has caused me.
Honestly, God I have tried, it is just not working.
Self.

RE: I can't let go
Dear self,
I understand letting go is hard especially when you are in the way. Take yourself out of the way and live according to the spirit by forgiving others the way I forgave you. If you forgive others, then your heavenly father will also forgive you of your sins (Matthew 6:15 NIV).
All the best,

God.

To: godmail.com
From: selfmail.com
Date 15th April 2020
Subject: I am carrying a heavy load

Dear God,
I have too much going on lately. I am frustrated and stressed up in life, sometimes I wish I were dead and gone, this is how serious it is. I have no friend now.

Please help me before something bad happens.
PS ugh! I look weird in the mirror. The good news is that I think I got skinner.

Love you,
Self.

RE: I am carrying a heavy load

Dear Self,
Cast all your cares upon me because I care for you. Take my yoke upon yourself for my yoke is easy and my burden is light. I know it is hard but carry your cross daily by continuing to abide in me so that a way out will be provided for you (Matthew 11:28-30 NIV).

I wish you all the best,

God.

To: godmail.com
From: selfmail.com
Date: 16th April 2020.
Subject: I received your gift.

Dear God,
I received the Jacket today; this Jacket was more than what I anticipated for and it came with a hoodie. It is so beautiful, and I would like to say thank you so much. I am so amazed.

I love you so much and it was worth waiting for. Sometimes, we wonder why we must wait for something so long and it is really something HUGE.

Best regards,
Self.

RE: I received your gift
I am glad you liked the gift I gave you. I just smiled. Now to him who can do immeasurably more than all we ask or imagine, according to his power that is at work within us. (Ephesians 3:20 NIV).
Enjoy your gift!

God.

To: godmail.com
From: selfmail.com
Date: 17th April 2020
Subject RE: RE: I received your gift

Did you say I liked it? I loved it and everyone is surprised that you gave me that Jacket (a bit envious I guess). Who cares? I am so rocking it.

Love Always,
Self.

RE: RE: RE: I received your gift

Dear Self,
I am happy that you are at rest.
Keep the light burning!

God.

To: godmail.com
From: selfmail.com
Date: 18th April 2020
Subject: I made up

Dear God,
I made up with my friend. I realized how unconditionally you have shown me perfect love, so I needed to give that love back unconditionally as well.

So, I went to her house and gave her a bear hug. She didn't resist at all because she had missed me as well. To be frank, we all missed each other. We did some catching up as well.

We took turns in riding her bicycle and it was so much fun!

Sincerely,
Self.

RE: I made up

Dear Self,
This is the best day of my life. I am so excited about this.
Happy? Understatement!

God.

To: godmail.com
From: selfmail.com
Date: 19th April 2020
Subject: Where is the love?

Dear God,
Yesterday, my friend showed a post of a little girl who had no place to call home. I was so sad the whole day. I really want to help her. I am thinking of sending her all my savings. She needs it more than I do.

Love,
Self.

RE: where is the love.

Dear Self,

I am so happy with the way you have grown to be so selfless. That is the essence of this relationship we have. To become like me stemming towards unconditional love.

God.

To: godmail.com
From: selfmail.com
Date: 20th April 2020
Subject: Praying Posture

Dear God,
What is the best posture to pray? I remember when I was younger, someone told me that the best way to pray for you to hear me was to fold my arms, bow down my head and close my eyes.
How true is that?

Respectfully,
Self

RE: Praying Posture
My dear, there is no posture to pray effectively. I hear every prayer no matter the position. All what matters is your heart. It just must be a heartfelt one. Just like what you are doing.

P.S. Pray according to the spirit all manner of prayers (Ephesians 6:18 NIV).

Love you endlessly,

God.

To: godmail.com
From: selfmail.com
Date: 21st April 2020
Subject: RE: PRAYING POSTURE

Dear God,
I am glad you made it clear on that. I get it now; all what matters is your heart! How simple.

How complicated people make the relationship with God to be?
I will forward your last email to my friend. She is struggling with that too.

XoXo
Self.

RE: RE: Praying Posture

Dear Self,
Tell your friend to send me an email me about all her confusion.
All the best,

God.

To: godmail.com
From: friendmail.com
Date: 22nd April 2020
RE: FW: RE PRAYING POSTURE

Dear God,
I don't know how the communication between you, and I stopped. I was not hearing you again and I felt you had left me.

Confused,
Friend
.

RE: FW: RE: PRAYING POSTURE

Dear Friend,
I am glad you reached out to me. We seriously have some catching up to do. Finding God is personal, just listen to your heart and what I tell you. Then you will no longer be infants, tossed back and forth by the waves, and blown here and there by every wind of teaching and by the cunning and craftiness of men in their deceitful scheming. In all things grow up to him who is the head, that is Christ (Ephesians 4:14-15 NIV). I am always with you.

FW: RE: PRAYING POSTURE
Dear God,

I am glad you made it clear on that. I get it now; all what matters is your heart!

How simple! How complicated people make the relationship with God to be? I will forward your last email to my friend. She is struggling with that.

XoXo
Self.

RE: RE: Praying Posture
Dear Self,
Tell your friend to send me an email me about all her confusion.
All the best,

God.

----- Forwarded Message -----
From: friend <friendmail.com>
To: "selfmail.com" <selfmail.com>
Sent: Wednesday, April 15, 2020, 10:02:40 AM EDT
Subject: RE: PRAYING POSTURE

From: godmail.com
To: selfmail.com
Date: 25th April 2020
Subject: Connect

Dear Self,

I have not been hearing from you lately, the more you commune with me, the more we get to know each other better for my will to be done in your life. Please connect. I love you so much.
God.
RE: Connect
Dear God,
I have been overwhelmed with issues at work. I get so busy that I really do not have time to talk to you. But guess what the harder I try to solve these issues, the worse it gets, and I become more frustrated. I am glad you sent me an email. I sure need you. Thank you for being a sweet daddy.
Self.
RE: RE: Connect

Dear Self,
I am happy you connected back to the vine. Take all your nutrients from the vine by abiding in me. That is the way you can be fruitful; apart from me you can do nothing. (John 15)
Best Wishes.

God

To: godmail.com
From: selfmail.com
Date: 26th April 2020
Subject: It is my birthday

Dear God,
I am so happy today, today is my birthday and guess what? I am throwing a little party at work. Amidst all my job issues, I am happy to be alive today and be able to share my birthday with others.

I had the cutest kitten today; the best part is that I didn't even ask for it. I named it Kittie. Mum thinks it is a weird name, but I think it is great.

With Love and Kittie
Self.

RE: It is my birthday!
Dear Self,

Not many people can celebrate their birthdays! You are blessed. Your heavenly father knows what you need before you ask him (Matthew 6:8 NIV).
Happy Birthday!
XOXO

God

P.S. Don't forget to send me pictures!

To: godmail.com
From: selfmail.com
Date: 27th April 2020
Subject: Why do you allow people to suffer?

Dear God,
I was talking to a colleague the other time. I heaped so many praises on you but to my dismay my colleague just cut in and said, "why will a loving God make people suffer?".

I need more information on this.

Sincerely,
Self.

RE: Why do you allow people to suffer?

Dear Self,

Unfortunately, suffering is part of the world we live in. God has not left us alone in our suffering. If we turn to Him, there is strength we never thought we could have. Also, there is comfort we never thought was possible and hope is restored. However, suffering produces perseverance and perseverance hope in Christ.

Faithfully,

God.

To: godmail.com
From: selfmail.com
Date: 28th April 2020
Subject: Loss

Dear God,

I am so downhearted today. My mum lost her baby and it is so devastating. The whole house is quiet. Daddy came back from peace mission immediately he heard the news. Do we still have to be thankful to you for not saving our little sibling?
P.S. I was hoping I would get a little sister to chat with and do all the girls' stuff. Are you sad that you took my sister away? Let me know.

Sincerely,
Self.

RE: LOSS

Dear Self,
I am so sorry for your loss. I wish it never happened, but sometimes certain things must be taken away for situations to be saved. She is at a better place now. In all circumstances, give thanks because this is the will of God in Christ Jesus (1 Thessalonians 5:18 NIV).
Sorry for your loss.
Sincerely,

God

To: godmail.com
From: selfmail.com
Date: 29th April 2020
Subject: Thanks

Dear God,

Thank you so much for your kind words. I was indeed comforted and guess what I have started comforting Daddy too in these trying times. He wonders where I got my strength from.

I fell from the stairs and broke my knee. Can you heal my knee?
Counting on your usual cooperation.

Thankfully,
Self.

RE: Thanks

Praise be to the God and Father of our Lord Jesus Christ, the Father of compassion and the God of all comfort, who comforts us in all our troubles, so that we can comfort those in any trouble with the comfort we ourselves receive from God. (2 Corinthians 1:3-4).
Expect your healing!

I love you,

God.

To: godmail.com
From: selfmail.com
Date: 30th April 2020
Subject: Update on my boss

Dear God,

My boss called me today into his office. Immediately, I entered I noticed his stern look. I looked straight into his eyes until he began to speak. He said, "you are different, I have never met anyone like you". he went on to ask me why? I told him Christ lives in me.
He wants to know about you.

Sincerely,
Self

RE: Update on my boss

Dear Self,
When Christ lives in you, the little light in you shines and people see your good works and glorify your father in heaven (Matthew 5:16 NIV).

Dare to be different.

Love you,

God.

To: godmail.com
From: selfmail.com
Date: 1st May 2020
FW: I am glad I found him.

Dear Self,

I have been able to find God and we talk every time. It is so much fun! I never knew what I was missing when I could not talk to him. He is such a wonderful companion.

I got to scoot to send God an email.
I love you Self.

Sincerely yours,
Friend

----- Forwarded Message -----
From: friend <friendmail.com>
To: "selfmail.com" <selfmail.com>
Sent: Wednesday, April 29, 2020, 1:02:40 AM EDT
Subject: I am glad I found him.

RE: FW: I am glad I have found him.
Dear Self,
Your friend and I have a wonderful relationship. I am a rewarder of those who diligently seek me. The Angels are rejoicing; a soul has been found. Amazing grace.
Sincerely,

God

To: godmail.com
From: selfmail.com
Date: 2nd May 2020
Subject: Vacation Over!

Dear God,

My vacation is over and so is my job. It was so awesome. My boss became nicer later (sorry, I forgot to tell you). I was enjoying it. He even wants me to work with him the next vacation. Thank you, God, for your advice, it was difficult initially obeying his instructions and doing the work, though, but once I allowed myself, for the Holy Spirit to take over, it was now the Holy Spirit doing it through me. It was fantastic.

My piggy bank is so full. I am sending money to the homeless girl.

Till then,
Self.

RE: Vacation Over!

I am so happy your vacation is over. Wow! See how time flies. Loving all people is the essence of living.

I am so proud of you girl!
KUDOS

God.

To: godmail.com
From: selfmail.com
Date: 3rd May 2020
Subject: Fulfilled

Dear God,
Ever since I met you and see the ever present help you give me all the time. I see my true self unfolding before my own eyes. As corny as it sounds, I now know who I am truly.
And I sincerely love myself.

Guess what?
All my friends in the girls group have all come back to me wanting to know you. They say I look composed now than ever. We are rebranding the girls' group. Our focus has changed, It's all about you Lord! We will chip in fashion along the line.

Best regards,
Self.

RE: Fulfilled

Dear Self,
Before you were born, I knew you. You are the salt of the earth. A city set on the hill that cannot be hidden (Matthew 5:13-16 NIV).

I love you so much!
God

The Lord is my Shepherd, I lack nothing.

Psalm 23:1 (NIV)

Adwoba Addo-Boateng

www.ingramcontent.com/pod-product-compliance
Lightning Source LLC
Chambersburg PA
CBHW050204130526
44591CB00034B/2127